Black Achievement IN SCIENCE
Engineering

Mason Crest

Black Achievement IN SCIENCE

Biology	Inventors
Chemistry	Medicine
Computer Science	Physics
Engineering	Space
Environmental Science	Technology

Black Achievement IN SCIENCE

Engineering

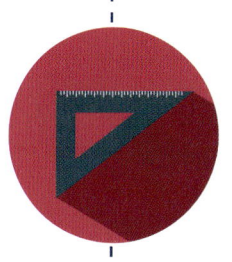

By MARI RICH

Foreword by Malinda Gilmore and Mel Poulson,
National Organization for the Advancement of
Black Chemists and Chemical Engineers

Mason Crest
450 Parkway Drive, Suite D
Broomall, PA 19008
www.masoncrest.com

© 2017 by Mason Crest, an imprint of National Highlights, Inc.

All rights reserved. No part of this publication may be reproduced or transmitted in any form or by any means, electronic or mechanical, including photocopying, recording, taping, or any information storage and retrieval system, without
permission from the publisher.

Printed and bound in the United States of America.

Series ISBN: 978-1-4222-3554-6
Hardback ISBN: 978-1-4222-3558-4
EBook ISBN: 978-1-4222-8325-7

First printing
1 3 5 7 9 8 6 4 2

Produced by Shoreline Publishing Group LLC
Santa Barbara, California
Editorial Director: James Buckley Jr.
Designer: Patty Kelley
Production: Sandy Gordon
www.shorelinepublishing.com

Cover photographs by PhotographerLondon/Dreamstime.

Library of Congress Cataloging-in-Publication Data
Names: Rich, Mari.
Title: Engineering / by Mari Rich ; foreword by Malinda Gilmore, Ph.D., Executive Board Chair, and Mel Poulson, Executive Board Vice-Chair, National Organization for the Professional Advancement of Black Chemists and Chemical Engineers (NOBCChE).
Description: Broomall, PA : Mason Crest, [2017] | Series: Black achievement in science | Includes index.
Identifiers: LCCN 2016002443| ISBN 9781422235584 (hardback) | ISBN 9781422235546 (series) | ISBN 9781422283257 (ebook)
Subjects: LCSH: African American engineers--Biography--Juvenile literature. | Engineers--United States--Biography--Juvenile literature.
Classification: LCC TA157 .R495 2017 | DDC 620.0092/396073--dc23
LC record available at http://lccn.loc.gov/2016002443

QR CODES AND LINKS TO THIRD PARTY CONTENT
You may gain access to certain third party content ("Third Party Sites") by scanning and using the QR Codes that appear in this publication (the "QR Codes"). We do not operate or control in any respect any information, products or services on such Third Party Sites linked to by us via the QR Codes included in this publication, and we assume no responsibility for any materials you may access using the QR Codes. Your use of the QR Codes may be subject to terms, limitations, or restrictions set forth in the applicable terms of use or otherwise established by the owners of the Third Party Sites. Our linking to such Third Party Sites via the QR Codes does not imply an endorsement or sponsorship of such Third Party Sites, or the information, products or services offered on or through the Third Party Sites, nor does it imply an endorsement or sponsorship of this publication by the owners of such Third Party Sites.

Contents

Foreword, by Malinda Gilmore and Mel Pouson, NOBCChE 6
Introduction 8
Elijah McCoy 10
David Nelson Crosthwait, Jr. 16
Otis Boykin 22
Hugh Robinson 28
Lonnie Johnson 36
Thomas Mensah 44
Walt Brathwaite 50
Careers in Engineering 56

Text-Dependent Questions 60
Research Projects 61
Find Out More 62
Series Glossary of Key Terms 63
Index/Author 64

Key Icons to Look for

Words to Understand: These words with their easy-to-understand definitions will increase the reader's understanding of the text, while building vocabulary skills.

Research Projects: Readers are pointed toward areas of further inquiry connected to each chapter. Suggestions are provided for projects that encourage deeper research and analysis.

Text-Dependent Questions: These questions send the reader back to the text for more careful attention to the evidence presented here.

Series Glossary of Key Terms: This back-of-the-book glossary contains terminology used throughout this series. Words found here increase the reader's ability to read and comprehend higher-level books and articles in this field.

Educational Videos: Readers can view videos by scanning our QR codes, providing them with additional educational content to supplement the text. Examples include news coverage, moments in history, speeches, iconic moments, and much more!

Science, Technology, Engineering and Mathematics (STEM) are vital to our future, the future of our country, the future of our regions, and the future of our children. STEM is everywhere and it shapes our everyday experiences. Science and technology have become the leading foundation of global development. Both subjects continue to improve the quality of life as new findings, inventions, and creations emerge from the basis of science. A career in a STEM discipline is a fantastic choice and one that should be explored by many.

In today's society, STEM is becoming more diverse and even internationalized. However, the shortage of African Americans and other minorities, including women, still exists. This series—*Black Achievement in Science*—reveals the numerous career choices and pathways that great African-American scientists, technologists, engineers, and mathematicians have pursued to become successful in a STEM discipline. The purpose of these series of books is to inspire, motivate, encourage, and educate people about the numerous career choices and pathways in STEM. We applaud the authors for sharing the experiences of our forefathers and foremothers and ultimately increasing the number of people of color in STEM and, more

By Malinda Gilmore, NOBCChE Executive Board Chair and
Mel Poulson, NOBCChE Executive Board Vice-Chair

Series Foreword

specifically, increasing the numbers of African American to pursue careers in STEM.

The personal experiences and accomplishments shared within are truly inspiring and gratifying. It is our hope that by reading about the lives and careers of these great scientists, technologists, engineers, and mathematicians, the reader might become inspired and totally committed to pursue a career in a STEM discipline and say to themselves, "If they were able to do it, then I am definitely able to do it, and this, too, can be me." Hopefully, the reader will realize that these great accomplishments didn't come easily. It was because of hard work, perseverance, and determination that these chosen individuals were so successful.

As Executive Board Members of The National Organization for the Professional Advancement of Black Chemists and Chemical Engineers (NOBCChE) we are excited about this series. For more than 40 years, NOBCChE has promoted the STEM fields and its mission is to build an eminent cadre of people of color in STEM. Our mission is in line with the overall purpose of this series and we are indeed committed to inspiring our youth to explore and contribute to our country's future in science, technology, engineering, and mathematics.

We encourage all readers to enjoy the series in its entirety and identify with a personal story that resonates well with you. Learn more about that person and their career pathway, and you can be just like them.

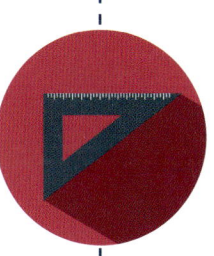

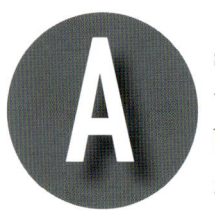sk most people what engineers do, and they will probably mention designing bridges or building tunnels. While that's correct, it's far from a complete answer. Engineering has many specialties, and engineers are involved in almost every facet of modern life. We brush our teeth with toothpaste formulated by chemical engineers, fly on planes tested by aerospace engineers, drink water whose purity is ensured by environmental engineers, and play video games designed by software engineers. Engineers work on the world's largest buildings and, smallest computer chips.

That tunnel? It took a whole team of engineers to envision, design, and build. A structural engineer decided how large it should be and what materials and equipment would be needed to build it; a mechanical engineer was responsible for its ventilation system; a civil engineer specializing in traffic issues gave advice about the posted speed limit and the rate at which cars should be allowed to enter and exit; and an electrical engineer designed its lighting system (because no one wants to drive through a dark tunnel).

Simply put, engineers are people who use science, technology, and math to come up with practical solutions to real-world problems. They strive to create a better world by making it safer, cleaner, healthier and much more efficient.

Many engineers are fond of quoting Albert Einstein, who once said, "Scientists investigate that which already is; engineers create that which has never been." Similarly, the novelist James Michener wrote in his 1982 book *Space*,

Introduction

"Scientists dream about doing great things. Engineers do them."

As they have done in every field of human endeavor, African Americans and people of African descent from around the globe have made enormous contributions to engineering—often in the face of equally enormous challenges. In this volume are profiles of just a few of the most well known individuals, representing many more achievers.

Despite that rich history, engineering still does not attract enough people of color. African Americans account for approximately 14 percent of the population, but the National Science Foundation has estimated that they represent just three percent of all scientists and engineers. It's imperative to change that situation because diversity is undeniably crucial to innovation. Scott E. Page, a professor of complex systems, writes, "Diverse groups of people [have] more and different ways of seeing a problem and, thus, faster [and] better ways of solving it."

The accomplishments of the men and women in this book are proof of that statement and can be inspirations to future engineers of color. Find out more about joining their ranks in Chapter 9.

Using existing machines or creating new ones, engineers are problem solvers.

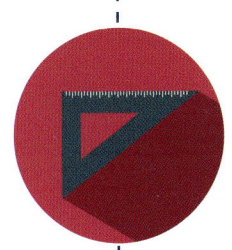

Words to Understand

apprenticeship
a period of learning a skill or trade from a master in the field

conduit
a channel for conveying water or other fluid

penchant
a strong or habitual liking for something or tendency to do something

Chapter 1

Elijah McCoy

Engineer and Inventor

Born:
Colchester, Ontario, Canada, c. 1843 or 1844

Died:
October 10, 1929, Detroit, MI

Nationality:
American, Canadian

Achievements:
57 U.S. patents, most to do with lubrication of steam engines

When a person refers to something as "the real McCoy," he or she is implying that the item is a genuine, high-quality piece of goods. Language experts disagree about the origins of the phrase, with some asserting that it is derived from an advertising slogan used by the Edinburgh-based MacKay whiskey distillery in the 1870s and others positing that American sportswriters first used it when discussing welterweight champion Norman Selby, who boxed under the name "Kid McCoy." (There is even another alcohol-related theory, which holds that the phrase stems from a Prohibition-era smuggler named Bill McCoy, who was known for procuring only the finest illegal liquor.)

Despite those admittedly colorful tales, the most widely accepted explanation is that the "real McCoy" was first used to refer to

 the revolutionary devices invented by engineer Elijah McCoy to lubricate steam engines. McCoy's innovations allowed for the engines to be lubricated while remaining in operation, eliminating costly and inefficient service stops. While steam engines eventually fell into disfavor with the development of the internal combustion engine, they were the major source of power for transportation and manufacturing in the 19th century, so McCoy's work had a major positive impact on the nation's economy.

There is some dispute about the exact date of Elijah McCoy's birth, but it was probably around 1843 or 1844. What is not in doubt is that his parents, George and Mildred Goins McCoy, had been slaves in Kentucky. With the help of the Underground Railroad, they escaped to Canada, where slavery had abolished in 1833.

Canada was then part of the British Empire, and a newly free and grateful George McCoy enlisted with the British military. In return for that service, he was granted 160 acres of farmland near Colchester, Ontario. Historians disagree—yet again—about the family's exact movements. Some say that when Elijah McCoy was about three years old, his parents returned to the U.S., settling with him and his eleven siblings in Ypsilanti, Michigan, on the north shore of Lake Erie. Others claim that the move did not take place until after the Civil War.

All agree, however, that Elijah McCoy showed a remarkable **penchant** for mechanics from a very young age and particularly enjoyed tinkering with farm machinery. When he was about 15, his parents, recognizing his intelligence and talent, arranged for him to travel to Scotland to undertake an **apprenticeship** in mechanical engineering.

Upon his return to Michigan, however, he found it impossible to find work as an engineer, despite his training and credentials. Although the Civil War had ended, racial prejudice was rampant, even in the North, and the only job he was offered was that of a fireman and oiler for the Michigan Central Railroad. His duties included shoveling coal at a rate of two tons an hour to fuel the steam engine and lubricate its moving parts; while some considered it an enviable job, because a fireman could sometimes be promoted to locomotive driver, it was backbreaking work—and a far cry from the more prestigious post for which he was qualified.

McCoy, like any engineer, particularly disliked inefficient systems, and he found it frustrating that the train had to be stopped frequently and the engine shut down before it could be oiled. He reasoned that it might be possible to pump oil to the spots at which it was needed with the help of steam pressure. Setting up a machine shop at his home in

Some antique engines still run on the power created by burning coal.

Elijah McCoy

Ypsilanti, McCoy created what became known as the lubricating cup, which consisted of a piston, set in an oil-filled container. Steam pressure pushed down on the piston, forcing the oil into **conduits** that carried it to the engine's moving parts.

McCoy received a U.S. patent on June 23, 1872, and the Michigan Central Railroad agreed to try the lubricating cup on some of its locomotives. The device was a resounding success, allowing for faster, more cost-effective train travel. The lubricating cup was later adapted to other types of steam engines and was widely used on ocean liners and in factory machinery. After others began making inferior knock-offs of the device, those in the know were said to ask for only the "real McCoy."

McCoy, who later moved to Detroit, received almost 60 patents over the course of his life—most for advanced, better-performing lubrication devices. (He said a device that allowed for the use of powdered graphite—an exceptionally effective lubricant but one prone to troublesome clogging—was among the most important of his innovations.)

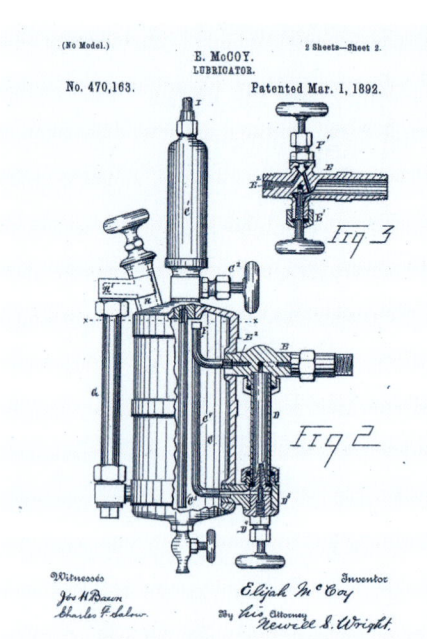

This is the drawing submitted by McCoy to the U.S. Patent Office for his most important railroad invention.

Because he lacked the funds to manufacture his own inventions, McCoy assigned most of his patent rights to outside investors or employers, who made millions of dollars from his talent and hard work. While that turn of events might have made some men bitter, McCoy was widely known as a kind figure, who could often be found showing his workshop to the children in his integrated neighborhood and encouraging all of them to study hard in school.

In 1920, when he was in his seventies, McCoy enlisted the help of a group of sympathetic investors and formed the Elijah McCoy Manufacturing Company to produce lubricators bearing his name. He had little time, however, to enjoy that accomplishment; suffering from both dementia and the long-term effects of a car accident that had killed his wife, Mary, in 1923, the engineer was admitted to the Eloise Infirmary in 1928 and died on October 10 the following year. It was not until 1975 that the city of Detroit placed a historic marker at the site of his home and named a street for him.

While newer technology has made his lubrication devices virtually obsolete, his name will always be synonymous with quality and solid workmanship.

Elijah McCoy and His Inventions

Words to Understand

fluid mechanics
a branch of physics that involves the study of liquids, gases, and plasmas and their reaction to forces acting upon them

thermodynamics
a branch of physics that deals with heat and related forms of energy

ventilation
the circulation of air within a closed space

Chapter 2

David Nelson Crosthwait, Jr.

HVAC engineer

Born:
May 27, 1898

Died:
February 25, 1976

Nationality:
American

Achievements:
HVAC executive, inventor, engineer, and author

Rockefeller Center is a complex of buildings in midtown Manhattan that covers more than 20 acres. Among its most famous structures is the Radio City Music Hall, the largest indoor theater in the world, with a marquee that stretches a full city block, an auditorium measuring 160 feet (48 m) from the back row to the stage, and an 84-foot (25-m) ceiling. Bringing the enormous complex to fruition posed the challenge of a lifetime for a host of architects, builders, and engineers. One of the most important of that group was David Nelson Crosthwait, Jr. Crosthwait, a mechanical engineer. He took on the task of designing Rockefeller Center's HVAC (Heating, **Ventilation**, and Air Conditioning) system, ensuring that millions of people each year can use the complex in comfort.

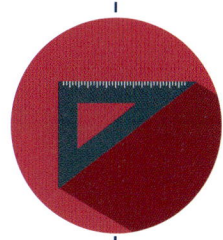

Crosthwait was born in Nashville, Tennessee, on May 27, 1898, and raised in Kansas City, Missouri, by parents who were widely respected members of that area's burgeoning black middle class. His father, David Nelson Crosthwait, Sr., had earned a degree from Tennessee's Meharry Medical College in 1891 and settled in Missouri four years later to teach physiology and chemistry at Lincoln High, an all-black school with famously rigorous academic standards.

Crosthwait's childhood coincided with a building boom in Kansas City, and several sparkling new skyscrapers, in-

As a child, Crosthwait would have enjoyed visiting Kansas City's Electric Park for rides and entertainment.

cluding the R.A. Long Building and the Scarritt Building, began dotting the landscape. (Perhaps even more thrilling to a child, in 1907 a large amusement park called Electric Park was constructed, and it was followed shortly thereafter by the Kansas City Zoo.) It was an atmosphere certain to excite the imagination of any aspiring young engineer, and that, coupled with his parents' emphasis on education, led Crosthwait to Purdue University, in Indiana. There he received a bachelor of science in 1913 and a master of engineering in 1920. (In 1975 the university would award him an honorary doctoral degree.)

After earning his bachelor's degree, Crosthwait—who had the deep understanding of **thermodynamics**, **fluid mechanics**, and heat transfer required to be an HVAC engineer—took a job with the C.A. Dunham Company, an Iowa-based manufacturer of high-end commercial heating and cooling systems. (It still exists and is now called Dunham-Bush.) At the company, where he remained until retiring in 1969, Crosthwait became known for his innovative work in the field of HVAC, and served as director of research there for several years. Some sources assert that without the indoor climate control technology that he helped develop at Dun-

The Scarritt Building, an early high-rise, still stands today in Kansas City.

Large buildings often have rooftop HVAC systems such as this one, which keep engineers busy.

ham, it would be virtually impossible to heat and cool massive buildings effectively.

Crosthwait wrote numerous journal articles on the topics of heat transfer, air ventilation, and central air conditioning, and he regularly revised sections of the *American Society of Heating and Ventilation Engineers Guide*, an important reference book. Within his field, he was also recognized for the sheer number of patents he earned—119 in all—for a wide variety of heating systems, vacuum pumps, refrigeration methods, and temperature regulators.

Crosthwait put some of his innovations to use when working on Rockefeller Center, which occupies the area between 48th and 51st streets in New York City and spans the long block between Fifth and Sixth Avenues. The complex was built during the height of the Great Depression by tycoon John D. Rockefeller, Jr., who felt that in those troubled times a project of that scope would serve as a symbol of optimism and can-do spirit. The "city within a city," as it was known during its construction, was declared a National Historic Landmark in 1987.

For his part in that project and others, Crosthwait was honored by the National Technological Association. In 1971, he became the first African American to be named a fellow of the American Society of Heating, Refrigeration, and Air Conditioning Engineers.

Crosthwait, who taught steam-heating theory and control systems at Purdue University after retiring from private industry, died on February 25, 1976, in West Lafayette, Indiana. In 2014 he was posthumously named to the National Inventors Hall of Fame. ●

Words to Understand

accreditation
to give official authorization to or approval of

rudimentary
involving basic principles

valedictorian
the student who has the highest grades in a graduating class

Chapter 3

Otis Boykin

Electrical engineer

Born:
August 29, 1920

Died:
1982

Nationality:
American

Achievements:
Electrical engineer, inventor, pioneer in resistors

It's easy to flick a switch on an electrical device without giving it much thought. Certainly few people would pause to consider that, upon turning on the television, that without devices called resistors controlling the flow of electricity through the circuitry, they would be watching a burnt-out screen instead of their favorite show. But whether we acknowledge it on a consistent basis or not, resistors make possible many of today's modern conveniences—and even some lifesaving innovations, such as the pacemaker.

Back in the mid-20th century, electrical engineer Otis Boykin was responsible for developing the resistors used in the modern pacemaker, as well as in numerous other products, including televisions and radios. They remain in use today—not only in entertainment products, but in computers,

guided-missile systems, and other important devices—and Boykin's contributions are still widely celebrated by anyone with even a **rudimentary** understanding of electrical engineering.

Boykin was born on August 29, 1920, in Dallas, Texas. His father, Walter, was a carpenter who became a minister later in life, and his mother, Sarah, was a homemaker. An exceptionally bright student, Boykin attended Booker T. Washington High, a local public school, and graduated as the class **valedictorian**. He subsequently won a scholarship to Fisk, one of the nation's top historically black colleges and universities. (The school had been established in 1865, right after the Civil War, in order to educate newly freed slaves, and it initially accepted students from ages seven to seventy. It was incorporated as an institution of higher learning two years later and in 1930 became the first African-American university to gain official **accreditation**.)

Upon graduating from Fisk in 1941, Boykin found a job as a lab assistant at the Illinois-based Majestic Radio and TV Corporation. (Its product labels featured an eagle, along with the motto "Mighty Monarch of the Air.") He ultimately worked his way up to lab supervisor and later accepted a post at P. J. Nilsen Research Laboratories, where he tested the automatic controls used in aircraft.

He next joined a mentor, Hal Fruth, in founding Boykin-Fruth Incorporated, which allowed them to collaborate on various research projects. Inspired in large part by Fruth, who held a doctoral degree, Boykin entered the Illinois Institute of Technology in 1946. He left the following year, however, before completing the requirement for a master's degree. Most sources assert that he could not afford the tuition, but Boykin himself has characterized that widely circulated tale as untrue. Speaking later in life to Julia Scott Reed, a writer for the *Dallas Morning News*, Boykin recalled that he had received an attractive job offer and simply did not have time to pursue further schoolwork.

In the middle of the 20th century, the field of electronics was undergoing rapid transformation. In 1947 engineers

Before Boykin and other inventors, most electronic machines were controlled by glass vacuum tubes such as these.

Otis Boykin

invented the transistor, which was much smaller and lighter than the vacuum tubes that had previously been used, and as a result, electronic devices got increasingly smaller. During the following decade, the integrated circuits were developed. An integrated circuit is an electronic circuit placed on a small piece of semiconducting material that performs the same function as a larger circuit made from multiple components. It was an exciting time, and Boykin was determined to make his own mark on it.

On June 16, 1959, he received his first U.S. patent, for a wire precision resistor. Resistors, as their name implies, impede the flow of electrical current, and Boykin's revolutionary device allowed engineers to designate for the first time a precise amount of resistance for a specific task. (While it may seem counterproductive to impede electrical flow, electrical engineers explain that it's necessary for many applications. Consider a simple toaster, for example. When the lever is pressed, an electric current flows through a filament; a resistor ensures that the current must "work," rather than travel freely, and that action heats the filament which in turn toasts the bread.)

Two years later Boykin was awarded another patent for an even more efficient and less costly resistor with the ability to "withstand extreme accelerations and shocks and great temperature changes without danger of breakage of the fine resistance wire or other detrimental effects." The U.S. military and consumer electronics manufacturers were soon clamoring for the resistors, which featured color-coded bands to indicate the level of resistance they provided.

Among the most important of Boykin's inventions was the control unit used in the modern pacemaker, a medical device that keeps a patient's heart beating at regular intervals by regulating it with electronic pulses.

Colored stripes allow engineers to identify the strength of resistors.

Boykin continued to invent throughout his life. In addition to his more well-known patented work, he developed a chemical air filter and a burglarproof cash register. Those products, however, were never made available commercially, and perhaps unsurprisingly were not considered as world-changing as his resistors.

Boykin, who lived for a time in Paris, died in 1982, but his contributions are a part of daily life around the world.

Words to Understand

regiment
a military unit generally consisting of several large groups (or battalions) of soldiers

Chapter 4

Hugh G. Robinson

Military engineer

Born:
August 4, 1932

Died:
March 1, 2010

Nationality:
American

Achievements:
US Army officer, engineer, commander of US Army Corps of Engineers

T he U.S. Army Corps of Engineers has its origins in 1775, when George Washington appointed the first engineer officers during the American Revolution. The U.S. Army established the Corps of Engineers as a separate, and permanent branch in 1802, but it was not until 1978—a wait of almost two centuries—that the Corps got its first African-American general officer: Hugh G. Robinson.

Hugh Granville Robinson was born on August 4, 1932, in Washington, D.C. His father, James Robinson, was a career army officer, and like many military families, the Robinsons moved often throughout their son's childhood. After graduating from Dunbar High, a predominately black school with a strong reputation for academic excellence, Robinson enrolled in the storied U.S. Military Academy at West Point.

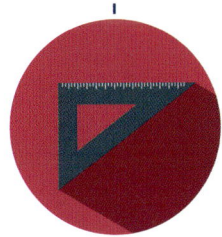

 Upon his arrival, he and three other black cadets were assigned to room together, segregated from the white cadets in their **regiment**. Shortly thereafter, however, a directive was handed down: the Corps of Cadets was ordered to more fully integrate, and Robinson got two new white roommates, with whom he remained close throughout their military careers. In 1954, upon completing the grueling academic, physical, and military training that comprises the

Cadets march at West Point, the US military academy where Robinson studied engineering, as well as military science.

Academy's curriculum, Robinson joined the Army Corps of Engineers as a second lieutenant.

Although many civilians are unaware of its existence, the Corps has long played an important role in the life of the nation. Throughout the 19th century, its engineers fortified the coasts, surveyed roads, mapped the Western frontier, built lighthouses and harbors, and constructed many of the buildings and monuments in the nation's capital. During the following century, the Corps took on the major responsibility for flood prevention and was instrumental in building facilities such as airfields and barracks that were needed during both World Wars. Corps engineers have undertaken large construction programs for federal agencies like NASA and the U.S. Postal Service; supported recovery efforts after the terrorist attacks of 9/11; dredged waterways to aid in the transport of goods and to provide recreation opportunities at national parks and campgrounds; and remediated toxic waste sites.

Robinson, who also completed an airborne course that trained him to use parachutes, served in South Korea from 1955 to 1956 and was promoted to first lieutenant during that period. Upon his return to the U.S. he attended the

The Corps of Engineers works on public projects such as this lighthouse in Maine.

 Massachusetts Institute of Technology (MIT), where he earned a master's degree in civil engineering in 1957. He subsequently steadily climbed the ranks of the Army Corps of Engineers. He was promoted to captain in 1960, while stationed in France; became head of the Combat Branch of the War Plans Division in 1963; and achieved the rank of major in 1964.

It was while Robinson was making plans to travel to Kansas to enroll in the Army Command and General Staff College at Fort Leavenworth that his superior officer explained that he was needed for a different assignment. Intent on receiving additional training, Robinson was resistant. Unaware of the nature of the assignment, he stubbornly continued to rebuff the officer until his father intervened, urging him to consider how his refusal might look on his record. Only after a still-reluctant Robinson agreed to take on the new post did he learn that he would be serving as a military aide to President Lyndon B. Johnson.

Robinson was the first African-American officer in that high-pressure role, which required him to handle all presidential correspondence relating to Army matters, to preside over the military aspects of visits by foreign leaders, and—perhaps most visibly—to act as a uniformed escort at presidential social events. In White House pictures from that era, his is often the only black face. Profiled in the November 1966 issue of *Ebony* magazine, he told the reporter, "To think that I had been chosen as the first Negro to become a military aide to a President of the United States, I was flabbergasted." Later, in 1968, when race riots broke out on the streets of Washington, Johnson sent Robinson out into the area to help defuse the tension.

Among his most difficult duties was to deliver Vietnam casualty figures to the president each day. When Johnson left office in January 1969, Robinson was determined to

Robinson (right) was part of many important meetings during his time in the White House with President Johnson (center).

"catch up" with his contemporaries, some of whom had already served multiple tours of duty in the escalating war. Promoted to the rank of lieutenant colonel, he served in Vietnam first as the executive officer of the 45th Engineer Group and then as commander of the 39th Engineer Combat Battalion.

Robinson returned in 1970 to Washington, to work in the War Plans Division at the Pentagon. He was promoted to colonel in 1973, and a year later, he was placed in command of the U.S. Army Engineer School Brigade at Fort Belvoir, a military installation in Virginia. After a subsequent stint as deputy director of civil works in the Office of the Chief of Engineers in Washington, in 1978 Robinson reached what could fairly be called the pinnacle of his career, when he was promoted to brigadier general and became the first African-American general officer of

The Pentagon in Washington DC is the world's largest office building.

Thomas Bostick is the current general of the Corps of Engineers.

the U.S. Army Corps of Engineers. (He would not be the last; indeed, the current Commanding General and Chief of Engineers is Thomas Bostick, who is also African-American.)

Robinson retired from the Army in 1983 with the rank of major general and numerous military honors, including the Distinguished Service Medal, Legion of Merit, Bronze Star, and Vietnamese Cross of Gallantry. He subsequently enjoyed a successful career in private industry, heading a series of Texas-based construction-management firms. A familiar figure in local philanthropic circles, he also sat on the boards of several museums and foundations, and he and his wife took care of more than a dozen foster children over the years.

Robinson died of congestive heart failure on March 1, 2010, after a long life of service as a soldier and engineer. ●

The Story of the U.S. Army Corps of Engineers

Words to Understand

eponymous
named after a specific person

Freon
the trademarked name of a group of chlorofluorocarbons used as aerosol propellants, refrigerants, and solvents

prototype
a preliminary model of an invention, especially a machine, from which other forms are developed or copied

Chapter 5

Lonnie Johnson

Aerospace engineer

Born:
October 6, 1949

Nationality:
American

Achievements:
Aerospace engineer, inventor, toymaker, entrepreneur

The millions of people around the world who have cooled off on a sweltering day by blasting each other with the high-pressure water guns known as Super Soakers® owe thanks to Lonnie Johnson, an engineer who got the idea for the popular plaything while trying to design an ecologically sound heat pump.

Johnson had a long road to travel before becoming a multimillionaire toy developer. The third of six children, he was born on October 6, 1949, in Mobile, Alabama—the heart of the Jim Crow South. His father, David, a veteran of World War II, worked as a driver, and his mother, Arline, as a laundress and nurse's aide; during the summers, they both toiled picking cotton.

From an early age Johnson, like many future engineers, enjoyed taking things apart

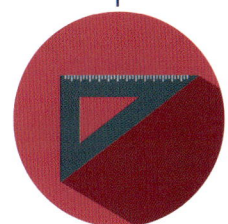

to discover how they worked (a process known as reverse engineering), and he once greatly upset his sister by dismantling her doll's head to study the mechanism that allowed its eyes to open and close. Because the family had little money to spare for nonessentials, he sometimes made his own toys, including a device he fashioned from bamboo shoots that could propel chinaberries, a pellet-like plant, through the air. Once, when he was a teen, he attached an old lawnmower engine to a cart built of scrap materials and zipped along a local road until he was scolded by the police.

Because Mobile was a segregated town, Johnson attended the all-black Williamson High School. Although Johnson was an exceptionally gifted student, his teachers—sadly aware of the racism and intolerance that he would face—advised him to aim for a low-level career as a technician. Johnson remained undaunted, however, pointing to the story of the iconic African-American inventor George Washington Carver as proof of the possibilities that might be open to him.

Like millions of others, Johnson was inspired by the achievements of George Washington Carver.

Johnson earned two degrees from Tuskegee, one of the leading historically black schools in the nation.

In 1968 Johnson, then a senior, represented Williamson High at the Alabama State Science Fair, held that year at the University of Alabama, Tuscaloosa. It was far from a welcoming place; just five years earlier, the state's infamously biased governor, George Wallace, had attempted to prevent black students from enrolling. Considering that recent history, it was perhaps unsurprising that Johnson was the only black student in the entire statewide competition. Still, his entry, a robot built of scavenged material and powered by compressed air, took first place, winning him a $250 cash prize and a plaque.

When Johnson graduated from Williamson High in 1969, he won math and ROTC scholarships to Tuskegee University, the renowned historically black school where George Washington Carver had once taught. (Williamson

High finally became integrated the year after Johnson left.) At Tuskegee he earned a bachelor's degree in mechanical engineering in 1973 and a master's degree in nuclear engineering two years after that.

Upon leaving Tuskegee, which would later award him an honorary doctoral degree, Johnson worked as a researcher at the Oak Ridge National Laboratory, which is run under the auspices of the Department of Energy. He subsequently joined the U. S. Air Force, and while in the military, he served as an acting chief of the Space Nucle-

The Oak Ridge Lab in Tennessee is one of America's leading nuclear power research facilities.

ar Power Safety Section at a weapons lab in New Mexico. Later, he was assigned to the Strategic Air Command (SAC) headquarters in Nebraska, and many sources credit him for his role in helping develop the stealth bomber program.

Johnson also worked at NASA's Jet Propulsion Laboratory in Pasadena, California, where he took on one of the most high-profile assignments of his career—working on the Galileo spacecraft. (Launched from the space shuttle Atlantis in 1989, Galileo arrived at Jupiter in 1995 and spent the next eight years circling that planet and sending back data.) Additionally, he served as the fault protection engineer during the early days of the Cassini spacecraft's mission to Saturn, a role that required him to ensure that no single systems failure would result in the loss of the entire craft.

Johnson worked on this *Galileo* spacecraft before it headed out to photograph and scan Jupiter.

While garnering many awards from the Air Force and NASA for his work, Johnson was not content unless he was also engaged in his own projects. One of his ideas was to create a heat pump that would use water instead of the pollutant **Freon**. One day in 1982 he was testing a **prototype** in his bathroom, and when he pulled the lever, a powerful stream of water shot across the room into his bathtub.

Johnson had never lost the playful spirit that had inspired him to motorize a homemade go-kart decades before. He immediately realized that he had stumbled upon a device that could make traditional squirt guns obsolete. After several years of tinkering to improve the design, he sold his idea to the Larami Corporation, which began mass-producing and marketing what they dubbed the Super Soaker in 1989.

The guns, which are manufactured by the toy giant Hasbro, soon became one of the most popular toys in the world and have generated an estimated $1 billion in sales.

Johnson, who was inducted into the State of Alabama Engineering Hall of Fame in 2011, now heads his own **eponymous** company, and he holds some 100 patents, including those for an innovative ceramic battery and an automatic sprinkler system. Among the most far-reaching of his projects is the Johnson Thermoelectric Energy Converter (JTEC), a heat engine that can efficiently and economically convert solar energy into electricity by splitting hydrogen atoms into protons and electrons. The JTEC, a self-contained unit that amazingly contains no moving parts, won the 2008 Breakthrough Award from the editors of *Popular Mechanics* magazine, and while the technology has attracted some naysayers, others feel it has the potential to transform the energy industry when it is fully developed.

Super Soaker Inventor Creates Advanced Power Generation

Johnson's award-winning invention came after many years of hard work and experimentation.

"Johnson will carve out a much greater place in history as one of the seminal figures of the ongoing green technology revolution," Paul Werbos, a former official at the National Science Foundation, has predicted. "This is a whole new family of technology. . . . It's like discovering a new continent. You don't know what's there, but you sure want to explore it to find out."

Words to Understand

polymer
a large molecule composed of many repeated subunits

Chapter 6

Thomas Mensah

Chemical engineer

Born:
1950

Nationality:
Ghanaian

Achievements:
Pioneer in fiber optics, inventor, entrepreneur, business leader

"Imagine technology so universal that it can circle the globe in seconds and influence the dynamics on land, sea and in the air," said an article in *Ebony* magazine. "Thanks to Dr. Thomas Mensah, you don't have to just imagine it. You can make long-distance calls using your cell phone, get your bank balance at any ATM in the world, or download an entire encyclopedia in a few minutes."

Mensah, a chemical engineer, is renowned for his part in advancing fiber optic technology, which allows data to be transmitted—quickly, reliably, and relatively inexpensively—through hair-like glass cylinders, thereby revolutionizing telecommunications and the Internet. Mensah explained to *Ebony* that fiber optics permeate everyday life. "The reason is that we communicate," he said. "We are social beings, so we've got to

communicate. Whether it's a land line or a cell phone line, fiber optics is the key ingredient that makes that communication possible."

Mensah was born in 1950 in Kumasi, a bustling metropolitan area in the Ashanti Region of Ghana. His father was a successful businessman who shipped cocoa products to chocolate manufacturers around the globe. Mensah was a precocious child, able to read the newspaper by age four, and thanks to the practice he got while conversing with his father's foreign business associates, he became fluent in French at an early age. (So proficient was he that he won *Le Grand Concours*, an annual competition sponsored by the

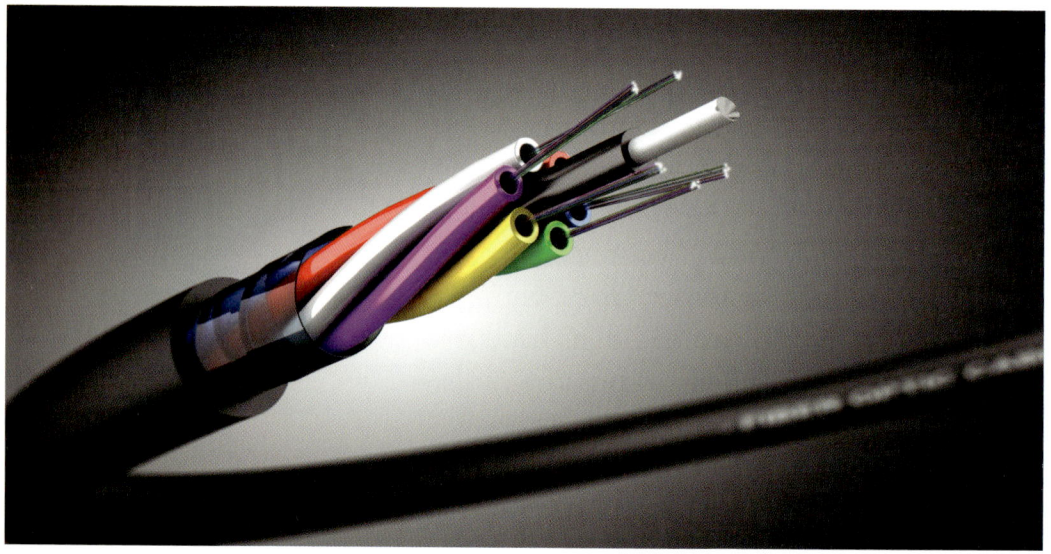

Groups of thin fiber-optic cables can be combined to transmit huge amounts of information in much less space than with copper wire.

American Association of Teachers of French, in both 1968 and 1970.)

At Adisadel College, a boys' boarding school in the town of Cape Coast, Mensah particularly excelled in science and math. Upon completing secondary school, he received a scholarship to study chemical engineering at the University of Science and Technology in Kumasi, where he also distinguished himself. In 1974 he was awarded a fellowship from the French government to study chemical engineering at the University of Science and Technology in Montpellier, and there he earned a doctoral degree in 1978.

While studying in Montpellier, Mensah had also participated in a program at the Massachusetts Institute of Technology (MIT), and in 1980 he returned to the U.S. to accept a job as a research engineer with a company named Air Product and Chemicals in Pennsylvania. He quickly entered company lore when he discovered that the simple step of altering the blade configuration on a mixing apparatus used in the manufacture of polyvinyl alcohol, a **polymer** used in the textile industry, resulted in a much higher quality product.

After three years in Pennsylvania, Mensah accepted a post at Corning Glass Works, in Upstate New York, a company at the forefront of developing the fiber optic technology that would make data transfer through copper cables a thing of the past. Before Mensah joined their team, Corning engineers had been unable to manufacture the exceptionally thin fibers without frequent breakage.

Within six months, Mensah had discovered that the

problem originated with the small bubbles that were being trapped in the polymer coating applied to the fibers. The bubbles weakened the glass, causing it to crack and slowing the manufacturing process. He found, however, that when carbon dioxide gas was injected in a layer of the coating, it prevented the bubbles from forming. His innovation allowed for the creation of much more durable fibers that could be produced 20 times faster than before and without breakage. At the time, copper wire was ten times cheaper than glass fibers (a dime per meter versus a dollar), but suddenly, the costs of the two products became comparable. The availability of Corning's newly affordable fiber optic technology made possible an Internet boom, as data traveled through bundles of the glass threads with unprecedented speed and efficiency. Anyone who has ever streamed a movie, sent a high-resolution photo, or gotten an answer from a search engine within seconds, owes those abilities in great part to Mensah.

In 1986, Mensah—who ultimately earned a dozen patents related to fiber optics—joined what was then called AT&T Bell Laboratories (later known as Bell Laboratories), where he used fiber optics to create a cutting-edge guided missile system, capable of working even when traveling at Mach 1—the speed of sound. The system incorporated a tiny camera within the missile's nose, which seamlessly transmitted images to the pilot,

Thomas Mensah, an African Innovator

who could then lock onto a target with great accuracy.

In 2000, Mensah founded his own firm, Georgia Aerospace Systems, where, working with nanoscale materials, he designs supersonic aircraft and other such vehicles. In 2009, while still heading Georgia Aerospace, he launched a second company, the Green Energy Corporation, which seeks to develop next-generation batteries for electric cars and other clean-tech solutions.

In 2014, Mensah was named a fellow of the National Academy of Inventors, a rare and important honor accorded to those "who have demonstrated a highly prolific spirit of innovation in creating or facilitating outstanding inventions that have made a tangible impact on quality of life, economic development, and the welfare of society," as the organization states on its website. He was the first person born in Africa to be inducted into the Academy.

The author of a 2013 memoir, *The Right Stuff Comes in Black, Too*, Mensah has announced his desire to build a "black Disneyland," with rides and attractions that would celebrate the history and achievements of people of color from around the world.

A lifetime of achievement led to Mensah being named to the National Academy of Inventors in 2014.

Words to Understand

organizational chart
a diagram that details the structure of a company and the relationships and ranks of its personnel and departments

U.S. National Bureau of Standards
a government agency founded to establish and promote the consistent use of uniform weights and measures, since renamed the National Institute of Standards and Technology (NIST)

Chapter 7

Walt Braithwaite

Engineering executive

Born:
c. 1943

Nationality:
Jamaican, American

Achievements:
CAD innovator,
aeronautics engineer,
Boeing executive

Decades ago, Boeing, the world's leading manufacturer of commercial airplanes, had a problem. Its designers and engineers, who were scattered around the world, were using a wide array of computer systems to create various parts for its products, making it difficult to standardize and collaborate. A young engineer from Jamaica, Walt Braithwaite, changed all that. Braithwaite developed a method for allowing computer-aided design and manufacturing systems (commonly referred to with the acronym CAD/CAM) to communicate, streamlining the process considerably.

"Engineers now are able to assemble entire planes down to the smallest of bolts and trap out any flaws before the actual model is built," Travis E. Mitchell explained in *US Black Engineer and Information Technology*

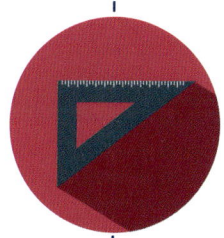

Magazine. "These innovations have saved millions of dollars in man-hours by cutting the research and development phase in half."

Braithwaite is a native of Kingston, Jamaica, although his family also lived for a time in Great Britain. His father took on any available job to support the family, repairing shoes and building cabinets at various points in his life, while his mother did the same, laboring as a seamstress and beautician. Braithwaite credits his work ethic to their strong example.

Braithwaite—who loved to dismantle his toys as a child, although he has admitted that he was not always able to put

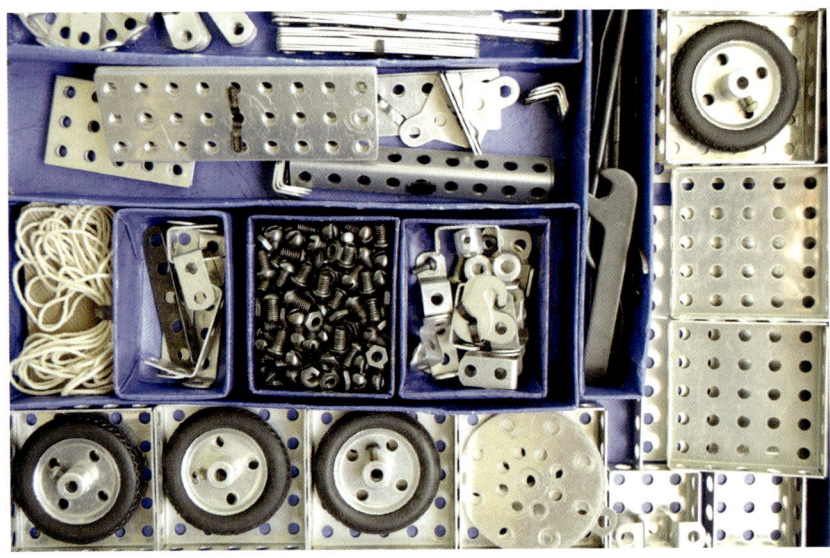

Braithwaite practiced his youthful love of mechanics and tinkering with kits of parts such as this one.

them back together—received what he has characterized as a good, British-style education. He took it upon himself to read every book on science and technology he could find in his local library, and while he was sometimes inspired to borrow a mystery, he rarely read anything so frivolous. He realizes that his background has given him an enviable advantage.

"People with that kind of ethic coming to the U.S., where there are so many opportunities, don't feel like there are many barriers [compared] to African Americans born here, who have to overcome barriers, who have been told [constantly] what they are not supposed to do," he said in a Seattle Times interview.

For college, Braithwaite traveled to Chicago to attend the American Institute of Engineering and Technology, where in 1965 he earned a bachelor's degree in engineering. Later he would receive a master's degree in computer science from the University of Washington.

Soon after completing his bachelor's degree, he was hired by Boeing as an associate tool engineer and assigned to the Fabrication Department. Although he was one of only a handful of black employees at the company, he asserted that he did not face racism. "You don't have to like me, though I would prefer if you did," he told the *Register-Guard*, an Oregon newspaper, while discussing his workplace attitude. "But if you respect me, I'll respect you, and we can do [the work] we need to do."

In 1975, Braithwaite was named a senior engineer and

This brightly decorated South African Airlines jet was one of many Boeing airplanes in use on the continent.

charged with discovering a standard format for the exchange of digital product data. The Initial Graphics Exchange Specification (IGES) that he helped develop was so useful that it was accepted in 1980 by the **U.S. National Bureau of Standards**.

His work revolutionized the way Boeing designed and manufactured its planes, beginning with the 777, which was the first jetliner entirely designed with a CAD program. Despite that incredible achievement, his advancement at the company seemed less than certain. Some managers considered him unaggressive to a fault, and he was typically the quietest person in any meeting. Still, after it dawned on officials that Braithwaite was quiet only because he was carefully considering solutions that were often simple, yet brilliant, he steadily rose up the corporate ladder. At the company's urging, he earned a second master's degree, this one in business management, from the Massachusetts Institute of Technology, and in 1985 was named director of computing systems in Boeing's Everett facility, where the 747 and 767 models were assembled.

In 1994, he was named vice president, with responsibility for all of the company's computer systems and intellectual property. The promotion placed him in a position of senior leadership, not far from the CEO on the **organizational chart**. The following year he was named 1995's Black Engineer of the Year by the Council of Engineering Deans of the Historically Black Colleges and Universities, Mobil Corporation and U.S. *Black Engineer and Information Technology Magazine*.

In 2000, Braithwaite was named president of Boeing Africa. The newly created post was meant to further the company's global reach, and Braithwaite took on an ambassadorial role, representing Boeing to African governments, businesses, and media outlets.

He retired three years later, in 2003, as the highest-ranking black executive in Boeing history.

An avid amateur sailor who once spent two years restoring a boat he had rescued from being junked, Braithwaite also spends much of his time tutoring and mentoring young people in a YMCA "Black Achievers" program, which provides academic support, career exploration, and character building.

Chapter 8

Careers in Engineering

Some people show signs from childhood that they are destined for a career in engineering, like Lonnie Johnson tinkering with old lawn mower parts to make a go-kart or Walt Braithwaite dismantling his toys to see how they worked. Others realized only later in life that they had the mix of creativity, intelligence, and desire to solve real-world problems that points to engineering. However they decide upon their goals, all successful engineers have at least one thing in common: a solid grounding in math and science.

Not everyone has to be like Thomas Mensah—a star student who went on to win academic scholarships and government fellowships—but everyone must plan in high school to take the courses that will adequately prepare them for their first rigorous year of engineering school.

It is best to take as many math courses as possible, including Algebra I and II, Geometry, and Statistics. Calculus is particularly important because many first-year college engineering courses assume a basic familiarity with the subject. It can be reassuring to keep in mind that while all engineers have a strong understanding of math, when they are faced with high-level mathematical issues they can call upon professional mathematicians and statisticians. Students should also take biology, chemistry, and physics, tackling advanced placement courses if their school offers them. (If not, some community colleges allow high school students to sign up for more rigorous classes.)

It takes more than science and math, however, to adequately prepare for engineering school. Because engineers must often communicate their ideas—to both other engineers and laypeople—language arts classes like writing and speech can also be important.

For those students who want to explore engineering outside of the regular academic year, many engineering schools around the country open their campuses in the summer for an array of exciting camps and programs. Participating in a summer program can be a good way to explore a col-

Virtually every engineering discipline calls for a solid grounding in higher math.

lege, meet current students and professors, and learn more about applying and attending. Many of the engineers profiled in this volume attended historically black universities and colleges because few other options were open to them, but today the choices are dizzying, and being on campus for a summer program can help ensure a good fit between school and aspiring engineer.

Engineering schools can be large or small and focused on cutting-edge research or teaching, but almost all can boast that they rank high on a measure called Return on Investment (ROI), which indicates that a student will graduate with good earning potential. Engineering has long been a path into the middle class for first-generation immigrants to the U.S. or other economically disadvantaged groups, and the cost of an engineering degree is widely considered to be money well spent. The U.S. Bureau of Labor Statistics estimates that a newly graduated engineer with a bachelor's degree can earn between $50,000 and $80,000 a year, depending on their area of specialization.

Salary, of course, is far from the only reason to choose a career, and most engineers—whether they work in research laboratories, construction sites, nuclear power plants, or any of the other places they can be found—feel that the best perk is the firm knowledge that they are making the world a far better place. ●

Partnering to Prepare Students for STEM Careers

Text-Dependent Questions

1. What type of engine caused the steam engine to fall into disfavor?

2. What does the V in HVAC stand for?

3. When was the transistor invented?

4. List three tasks in which the U.S. Army Corps of Engineers has been involved.

5. What did Lonnie Johnson make from bamboo when he was a child?

6. What happened when Corning engineers initially tried to manufacture exceptionally thin glass fibers?

7. What was the first jetliner entirely designed with a CAD program?

Suggested Research Projects

1. Some people still build steam engines for fun. Go online and search for instructions for building a simple steam engine. What special skills or tools would be needed?

2. HVAC engineers must understand the laws of thermodynamics. Look them up. Can you think of everyday examples that demonstrate the laws?

3. Pacemakers are continually being refined and improved. Make a timeline listing the major changes made to the device throughout the years. When did they become portable? When was the first implantable pacemaker developed?

4. The U.S. Army Corps of Engineers is responsible for flood prevention. Explore what methods they use. Are they always successful?

5. Many people would like to avoid Freon because it's considered a pollutant. Look up its benefits and dangers.

6. Fiber optic cables come in various widths. Research the uses for fibers of varying widths.

7. There are many free CAD programs available. Try downloading one and using it to create a drawing.

Find Out More

Websites

www.nacme.org
National Action Council for Minorities in Engineering. This group is devoted to developing an "engineering workforce that looks like America." The website includes information on careers, college aid, and more.

www.nsbe.org
The National Society of Black Engineers. This membership organization provides useful information for students, parents, and teachers.

www.bls.gov
The U.S. Bureau of Labor Statistics. This government site publishes descriptions and starting salaries for a wide variety of engineering careers.

TryEngineering.org
A joint effort between the Institute of Electrical and Electronics Engineers, IBM, and the New York Hall of Science to provide a highly comprehensive resource on engineering and engineering careers, including lists of schools, summer programs, and internships.

Books

Andrews, Beth. *Hands-On Engineering*. Waco, TX: Prufrock Press, 2012.
This book prompts students to understand design and engineering as they create innovative solutions to challenges. Challenges in the book let students solve real-world problem hands-on.

Landis, Raymond B. *Studying Engineering: A Road Map to a Rewarding Career*. Los Angeles: Discovery Press, 2013.
This book's fourth edition includes sections on reverse engineering, sustainability, lifelong learning, studying abroad, entrepreneurship, teamwork and leadership, and engineering ethics.

Series Glossary of Key Terms

botany the study of plant biology

electron a negatively charged particle in an atom

genome all the DNA in an organism, including all the genes

nanometer a measurement of length that is one-billionth of a meter

nanotechnology manipulation of matter on an atomic or molecular scale

patent a set of exclusive rights granted to an inventor for a limited period of time in exchange for detailed public disclosure of an invention

periodic table the arrangement of all the known elements into a table based on increasing atomic number

protein large molecules in the body responsible for the structure and function of all the tissues in an organism

quantum mechanics the scientific principles that describe how matter on a small scale (such as atoms and electrons) behaves

segregated separated, in this case by race

ultraviolet a type of light, usually invisible, that can cause damage to the skin

Index

aerospace engineering 41, 42, 49, 51, 53
Boeing 51, 53, 54, 55
Boykin, Otis 23-27
Braithwaite, Walt 51-55
Carver, George Washington 38, 39
chemical engineering 45, 47, 49
Civil War 13, 24
Corning Glass Works 47
Crosthwait, David Nelson Jr. 17-21
electrical engineering 23, 24, 26
Einstein, Albert 8
Electric Park 18, 19
Georgia Aerospace Systems 49
Ghana 45, 6, 47
HVAC 17, 19
inventions, 13, 14, 26, 27, 41, 42, 48
Jet Propulsion Lab 41
Johnson, Lonnie 37-43
Johnson, President Lyndon 32, 33
Massachusetts Institute of Technology 32, 47
Mensah, Thomas 45-49
McCoy, Elijah 11-15
Michigan Central Railroad 14
NASA 41
National Inventors Hall of Fame 21
National Science Foundation 9, 43
Oak Ridge Lab 40
Pentagon 34
Purdue University 21
railroads 13, 14
resistors 23, 26, 27
Robinson, Hugh G. 29-33
Rockefeller Center 17, 20, 21
Rockefeller, John D. 21
STEM careers 6-7, 8-9, 57, 58, 59
SuperSoakers 37, 42
Tuskegee University 39, 40
US Army Corps of Engineers 29, 31, 34 ,35
US Military Academy 29, 30, 31
Vietnam War 33, 34

Photo credits

AP Photo/Atlanta Journal-Constitution/Jessica McGowan 36. Dreamstime.com: Monkey Business 9, Thomas Marchart 10, Jiawangkun 16, Olivier Le Queinec 20, Ryan Carter 22, intheflesh 25, Riverrail 27, Ivan Cholakov 34, Colour59 37, Nikkytok 44, Olivier Le Moal 46, Lizapolina 52, Michael Zhang 56, Andrey Popov 58. Johnson Battery Technologies: 43. Lyndon Johnson Presidential Library: 33. National Academy of Inventors: 49. Newscom: Jim Bryant/UPI 50. Shutterstock: Chris Jenner 13, Joseph Sohm 30. US Army Corps of Engineers: 28, 29, 35. USDA: 38. US Parks Department: 39. US Deparment of Energy: 40. NASA: 41. Wikimedia: Mwkruse 19, Montague Smith 55

About the Author

Mari Rich was educated at Lehman College, part of the public City University of New York. As a writer and editor, she has had many years of experience in the fields of university communications and reference publishing, most notably with the highly regarded periodical *Current Biography*, aimed at high school and college readers. She also edited and wrote for *World Authors, Leaders of the Information Age*, and *Nobel Laureates*. Currently, she spends much of her time writing about engineers and engineering.